FUN & CREATIVE
WORKSHOP ACTIVITIES

COOL
ENGINEERING
PROJECTS

REBECCA FELIX

**Checkerboard
Library**

An Imprint of Abdo Publishing
abdopublishing.com

ABDOPUBLISHING.COM

Published by Abdo Publishing, a division of ABDO, PO Box 398166, Minneapolis, Minnesota 55439. Copyright © 2017 by Abdo Consulting Group, Inc. International copyrights reserved in all countries. No part of this book may be reproduced in any form without written permission from the publisher. Checkerboard Library™ is a trademark and logo of Abdo Publishing.

Printed in the United States of America, North Mankato, Minnesota
062016
092016

THIS BOOK CONTAINS
RECYCLED MATERIALS

Design and Production: Mighty Media, Inc.
Series Editor: Paige V. Polinsky
Photo Credits: Rebecca Felix, Paige V. Polinsky, Shutterstock

The following manufacturers/names appearing in this book are trademarks: DeWALT®, Duracell®, Duro®, Energizer®, Sharpie®

Library of Congress Cataloging-in-Publication Data

Names: Felix, Rebecca, 1984- author.
Title: Cool engineering projects : fun & creative workshop activities / Rebecca Felix.
Description: Minneapolis, Minnesota : Abdo Publishing, [2017] | Series: Cool industrial arts | Includes index.
Identifiers: LCCN 2016006311 (print) | LCCN 2016009416 (ebook) | ISBN 9781680781274 (print) | ISBN 9781680775471 (ebook)
Subjects: LCSH: Engineering--Juvenile literature. | Engineering--Experiments --Juvenile literature. | Science projects--Juvenile literature.
Classification: LCC TA149 .F45 2017 (print) | LCC TA149 (ebook) | DDC 620.1--dc23
LC record available at http://lccn.loc.gov/2016006311

TO ADULT HELPERS

This is your chance to help children learn about industrial arts! They will also develop new skills, gain confidence, and make cool things. These activities are designed to teach children about engineering. Readers may need more assistance for some activities than others. Be there to offer guidance when they need it. Encourage them to do as much as they can on their own. Be a cheerleader for their creativity!

Look at the beginning of each project for its difficulty rating (EASY, INTERMEDIATE, ADVANCED).

TABLE (OF) CONTENTS

WHAT IS ENGINEERING?

Did you know you are surrounded by engineering **marvels**? Every car, bus, bridge, and building is a product of engineering! Engineering is designing and building structures, machines, and products using science, math, and technology. It has existed for thousands of years. Ancient Egyptian engineers built giant pyramids. Ancient Greek and Roman engineers constructed famous temples. Many of these ancient structures are still standing today!

ENGINEERING TECHNIQUES

Workshop Tips

It is important to set up a safe workshop before beginning any engineering project. Your workshop should have a flat, hard surface. It could be in the garage, in the basement, or at the kitchen table. Just make sure you get **permission**! Then, follow the tips below to work safely.

- Always cut on top of a thick cutting board or piece of scrap wood.

- Always wear gloves made of leather or cotton with rubber padding when handling metal with sharp edges.

- Wear safety goggles when cutting wood or metal.

- Work in a well-**ventilated** area when gluing.

- Wear a face mask when using strong glues or handling floral foam. The foam gives off a fine dust.

- Always get adult help when using knives. And always cut away from your body.

Essential Safety Gear

- Gloves

- Safety goggles

- Face mask

- Closed-toe shoes

Be Prepared

- Read the entire project before you begin.

- Make sure you have everything you need to do the project.

- Follow the directions carefully.

- Clean up after you are finished.

ADULT HELPERS

Engineering can be **dangerous**. Metal pieces can have sharp edges. The tools used to cut and shape metal can also be sharp. That means you should have an adult standing by for some of these projects.

KEY SYMBOLS

In this book, you may see one or more symbols at the beginning of a project. Here is what they mean:

SUPER SHARP!
A sharp tool is needed. Get help!

HOT!
This project requires hot tools. Handle with caution.

SAFETY GOGGLES
Eye protection should be worn for certain steps in this project.

FACE MASK
Doing this project creates dust or requires glues with strong odors. A face mask should be worn for protection.

TOOLS OF THE TRADE

Here are some of the materials you will need for the projects in this book.

CERAMIC MAGNETS   COPING SAW   CRAFT KNIFE   CRAFT STICKS

FABRIC   FLORAL FOAM BRICK AND MUG PLUG   MARKER   NEEDLE-NOSE PLIERS

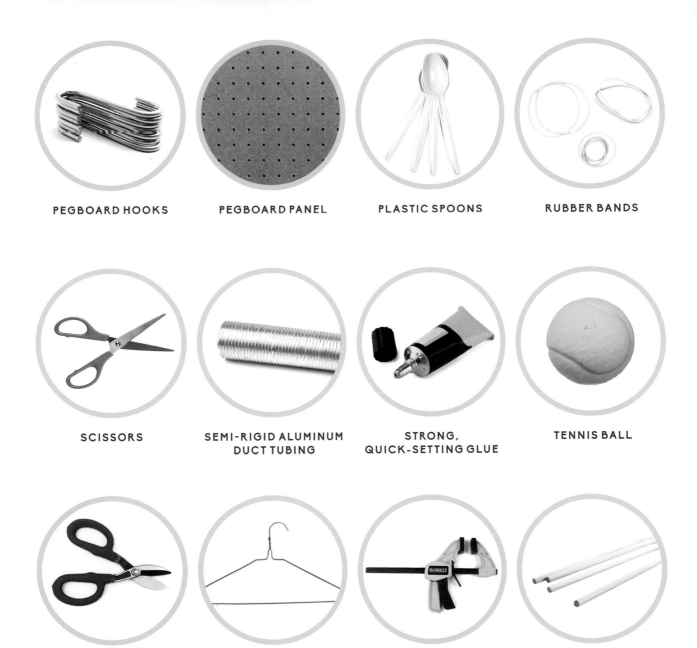

PEGBOARD HOOKS

PEGBOARD PANEL

PLASTIC SPOONS

RUBBER BANDS

SCISSORS

SEMI-RIGID ALUMINUM DUCT TUBING

STRONG, QUICK-SETTING GLUE

TENNIS BALL

TIN SNIPS

WIRE HANGER

WOOD CLAMP

WOODEN DOWELS

TWISTING TUBE RACE TUNNEL

BUILD A TWISTY TRACK THAT HANGS FROM A DOOR!

MATERIALS

- 2 pieces of semi-rigid aluminum duct tubing, 3″ × 8″ (7.5 × 20 cm)
- aluminum tape
- needle-nose pliers
- wire hanger
- tennis ball
- wood clamp
- scrap wood or cutting board
- craft knife
- washers, marbles, or other small weights
- strong, quick-setting glue
- stopwatch
- ping-pong ball
- bouncy ball
- large marble

MAKING THE TWISTING TUBE

1 Gently stretch out both **aluminum** tubes.

2 Tape the ends of the tubes together.

3 Use the pliers to bend the hanger into a long, skinny oval shape. Leave the hanger's hook **intact**.

Continued on the next page.

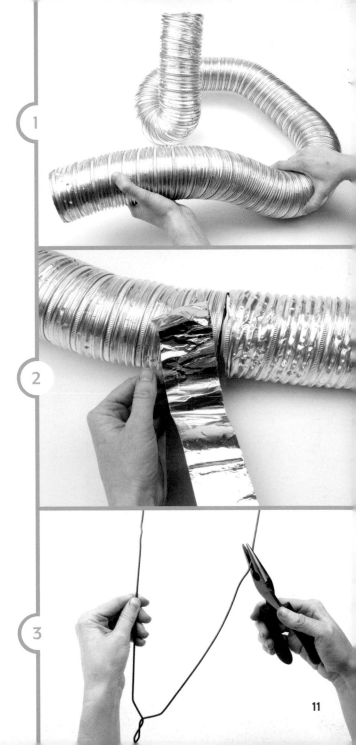

11

4 Thread one end of the tube through the hanger. Fit the tube snug against the hanger's curve. Tape the hanger to the tube.

5 Hang the tube on the top of a door using the hanger's hook. Bend and twist the tube into curves and loops until it reaches the floor.

MAKING + RACING
THE BALLS

1 Alter your tennis ball to make it extra heavy. Clamp the ball to the scrap wood or cutting board. Have an adult cut a small slit in the ball using the knife.

2 Fill the ball with several small weights. Then glue the slit together and let dry.

3 Drop the weighted tennis ball down your structure. Time how long it takes to reach the bottom. Then time the other balls you gathered. Which is fastest? Which is slowest? Why do you think that is?

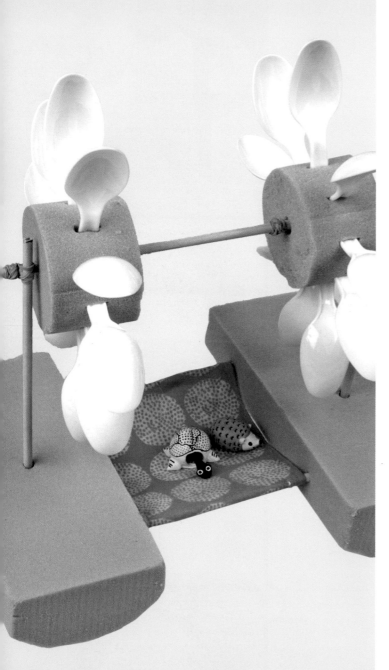

WIND ROTOR CATAMARAN

POWER A FOAM BOAT WITH SPINNING SPOON WHEELS!

MATERIALS

- craft knife
- 2 floral foam bricks, 3" × 4" × 8" (7.5 × 10 × 20 cm)
- cutting board
- ruler
- marker
- wooden dowel, ³⁄₁₆" × 36" (0.5 × 91.4 cm)
- coping saw
- scissors
- fabric
- hot glue gun & glue sticks
- 2 to 4 binder clips
- floral foam mug plug, 3" × 4" (7.5 × 10 cm)
- drinking straw
- tin snips
- 16 to 20 plastic spoons
- several rubber bands
- bathtub
- water
- blue food coloring (optional)

MAKING THE BOAT

1 Carve one wide side of a foam brick into a shallow U shape. Repeat with the other brick. These will be the **hulls**.

2 Have an adult help you saw two pieces of dowel 6½ inches (16.5 cm) long. Set the hulls next to each other, curved sides down. Push one end of each dowel into the side of one hull. Push the other end of each dowel into the other hull.

3 Cut a rectangular piece of fabric as wide as the space between the hulls. Make it a little longer than the space between the dowels. Hot glue the fabric to the dowels. Clip it in place while the glue dries.

Continued on the next page.

15

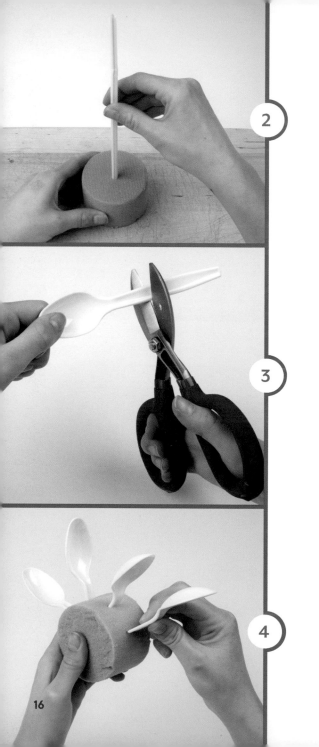

MAKING THE WIND ROTORS

1 Slice the foam plug in half to make two **cylinders**.

2 Use a straw to punch a hole through the center of each cylinder.

3 Put on the safety goggles. Use the tin snips to shorten the spoon to 1 to 2 inches (2.5 to 5 cm).

4 Push 8 to 10 spoons into the curved side of one cylinder. Space them evenly apart. Make sure all spoon heads face the same direction.

5 Repeat step 4 with the other cylinder. You now have two **rotors**!

ATTACHING THE ROTORS

1 Have an adult help you saw a piece of dowel 10 inches (25.4 cm) long.

2 Wrap two rubber bands around the dowel. Space them several inches in from each end.

3 Thread a **rotor** onto one end of the dowel. Make sure the rotor spins freely. If it doesn't, push the straw into the hole and wiggle it around a bit.

Continued on the next page.

TIP
The shortened handles don't need to be exact! Measure and cut the first one. Cut the rest using the first one as an example.

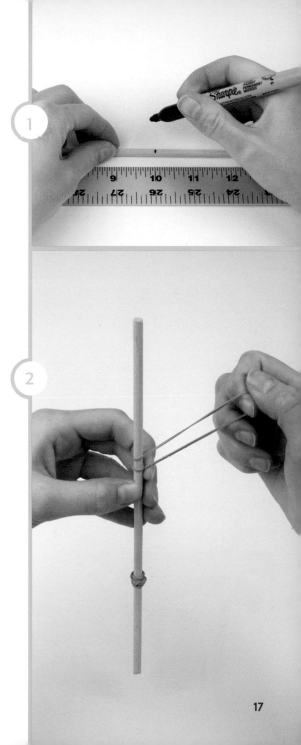

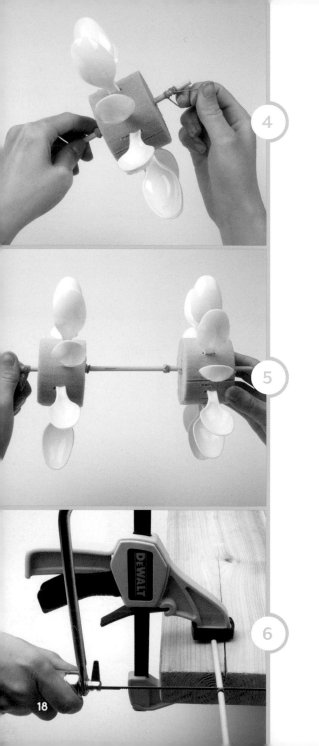

4 Wrap a rubber band around the end of the dowel. It should be close to, but not touching, the foam. This will keep the **rotor** on the dowel.

5 Repeat steps 3 and 4 on the other end of the dowel with the other rotor. Thread the second rotor so its spoons face the same direction as the first.

6 Have an adult help you saw one of the dowels in half.

TIP
Add one drop of blue food coloring to the water in your tub. This will make it look as though your **catamaran** is sailing on the sea!

7 Set the boat down with the curved **hulls** facing down. Push a dowel into the center of each hull.

8 Attach the ends of the **rotor** dowel to the ends of the standing dowels. Wrap rubber bands around the dowels to connect them.

9 Fill the tub with a few inches of water. Set your boat in the water with the spoon fronts facing you. Use the straw to blow on the spoons. Then watch your ship sail away! If it's windy outdoors, find a pond and let the wind do the work!

19

AIRPLANE CATAPULT + TARGET

CONSTRUCT A CATAPULT AND SEND A PLANE SOARING!

MATERIALS

- newspaper
- 5 craft sticks
- acrylic paint
- paintbrush
- 25 to 30 rubber bands, 3" by ⅛" (7 × 0.3 cm)
- strong, quick-setting glue
- 2 ceramic magnets
- 11 wooden dowels, ¼" × 12" (0.6 × 30.5 cm)
- binder clips
- 7" (17.8 cm) rubber band
- ruler
- marker
- wooden dowel, ⅜" × 18" (1 × 45.7 cm)
- paper
- refrigerator
- refrigerator magnet

BUILDING THE PLANE

1 Cover your work surface with newspaper. Paint the craft sticks fun colors. Let them dry.

2 Stack two craft sticks together. Place them between two more craft sticks, making a *t* shape. Use a rubber band to hold them in place.

3 The outer craft sticks are the plane's wings. Glue one magnet to the end of each wing.

Continued on the next page.

21

BUILDING THE CATAPULT

1 Paint the dowels fun colors. Let them dry.

2 Use rubber bands to connect four short dowels to make a square. Wrap the rubber bands around the ends of the dowels until they are connected securely.

3 Connect a short dowel, standing vertically, inside one corner of the square. Connect another short dowel to the square inside a neighboring corner.

4 Connect two short dowels to the other two corners, but on the outside of the square.

5 Cross the tops of an inside dowel and an outside dowel to form a triangle. Use a rubber band to connect them. Repeat with the other two short dowels.

6 Place a short dowel across the tops of the triangles. Secure with rubber bands.

7 On a non-triangle side, make an X with two short dowels. Make sure its cross isn't higher than halfway up the vertical dowels. Use binder clips to hold the dowels in place.

8 Connect the X to the vertical dowels with rubber bands.

Continued on the next page.

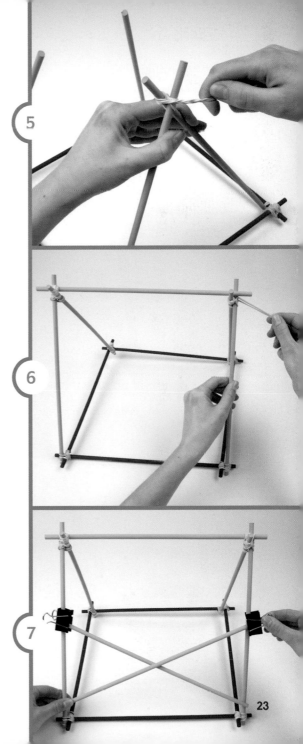

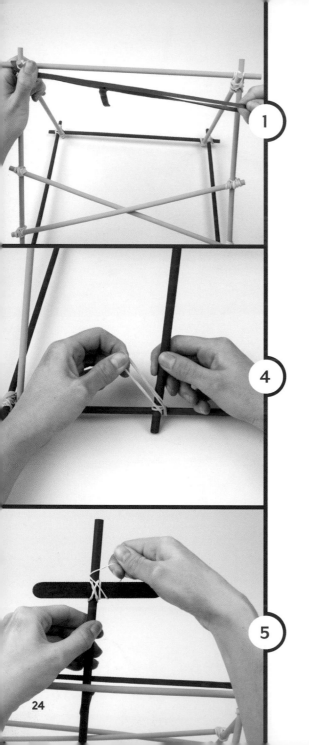

MAKING + ATTACHING THE ARM

1 Hook the long rubber band over the top dowels on the X side of the structure.

2 On the side opposite the X, find the middle of the base. Make a small mark.

3 Slide the long dowel between the **horizontal** dowel and long rubber band.

4 Use a rubber band to attach the end of the long dowel to the base at the mark. This is the catapult's arm.

5 Use a rubber band to attach a craft stick across the arm near the top.

MAKING THE TARGET + TAKING AIM!

1 Paint a target on paper. Let it dry.

2 Hang the target on your refrigerator with a magnet. Set your catapult up in front of the refrigerator.

3 Hold the plane against the catapult arm. The plane's magnets should be facing out. Pull the arm back, stretching the large rubber band. Take aim at the target and let it go!

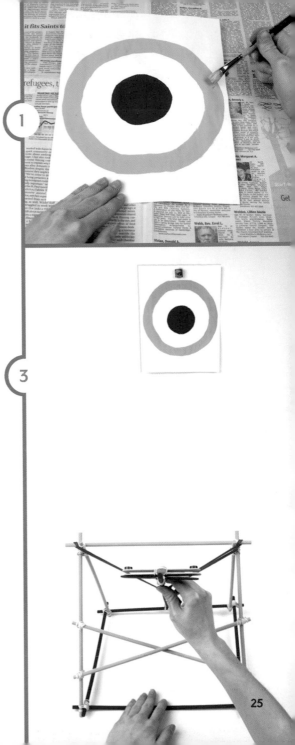

TUBE + TUMBLE
MAZE

ARRANGE WHEELS,
PULLEYS, TUBES, PEGS,
AND MORE TO CREATE
A PEGBOARD MAZE!

MATERIALS

- old towel
- pegboard panel, ¼"× 2' × 4' (0.6 cm × 0.6 m × 1.2 m)
- acrylic paint
- paintbrushes
- floral foam mug plug
- cutting board
- craft knife
- drinking straws
- tin snips
- 16 to 20 plastic spoons
- paper towel and toilet paper tubes
- scissors
- floral foam brick
- empty water bottle
- stapler
- semi-rigid aluminum duct tubing
- aluminum tape
- pegboard hooks
- golf ball
- marker (optional)

DECORATE THE BOARD

I Place an old towel beneath the pegboard to protect your floor. Paint the pegboard fun colors or with a design.

FOAM + SPOON WHEELS

I Cut the foam plug in half to make two short **cylinders**. Use a straw to make a hole through the middle of each cylinder.

2 Put on the safety goggles. Use tin snips to shorten the plastic spoon handles. Push 8 to 10 spoons into the curved side of each cylinder. Space them evenly apart. Make sure all spoon heads face the same direction.

Continued on the next page.

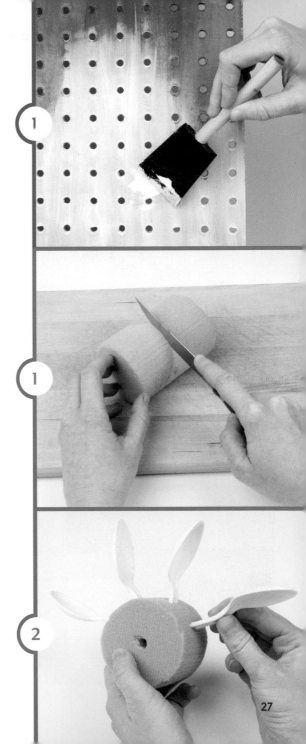

27

CARDBOARD RAMPS

1 Cut paper towel and toilet paper tubes in half lengthwise. Paint them fun colors.

SQUARE FOAM WHEELS

Cut a floral foam brick into small bricks.

2 Use a straw to make a hole through the middle of each brick.

TURN YOUR MAZE INTO A GAME!

Divide the bottom quarter of the board into three sections. Make each section a different size. Paint them different colors.

Number the sections. Write "1" in the biggest section, "2" in the medium-sized section, and "3" in the smallest section.

When the ball reaches the bottom of the maze, give the player the number of points written on the section where it landed.

WATER-BOTTLE WHEEL

1 Have an adult help you cut the ends off an empty water bottle. This makes a clear tube.

2 Cut the tube into several smaller tubes. Then cut all but one tube into two curved pieces.

3 Staple the small curved pieces to the **intact** tube. Make sure all the pieces face the same direction.

Continued on the next page.

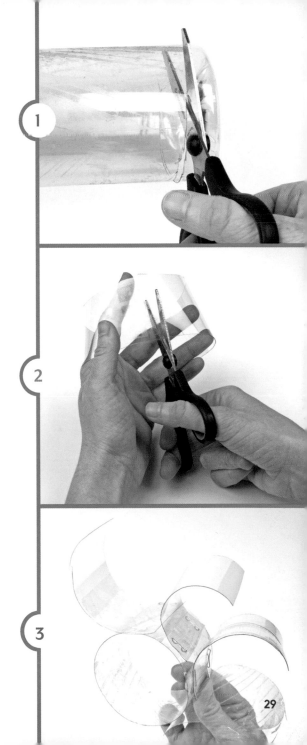

29

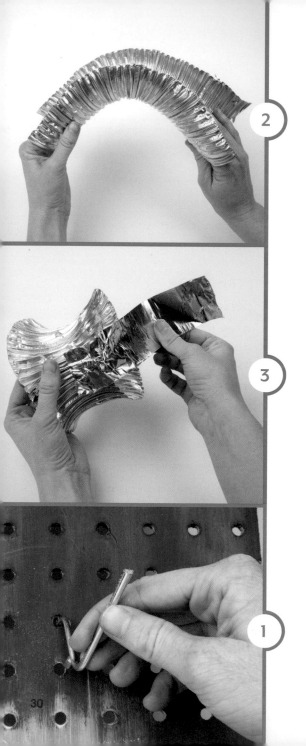

ALUMINUM TUBING WHEELS

1 Cut a short **cylinder** out of the **aluminum** tubing. Cut the cylinder in half lengthwise.

2 Bend one piece of the cut tubing into a circle.

3 Tape the ends together. Repeat with the other piece of cut tubing.

HANGING HOOKS + CREATING THE MAZE

1 Hang the hooks in the pegboard to hold the obstacles. Arrange them so you can start a ball at the top and it will hit the obstacles on the way to the bottom.

2 Drop the golf ball at the top of your maze. Does it roll and run through all the obstacles as you imagined? Rearrange, remove, or add to the maze to make new paths!

GLOSSARY

ALUMINUM – a silver-colored, lightweight metal. It is used in making machinery and other products.

CATAMARAN – a boat that has two hulls.

CYLINDER – a solid bounded by two parallel circles and a curved surface. A soda can is an example of a cylinder.

DANGEROUS – able or likely to cause harm or injury.

HORIZONTAL – in the same direction as the ground, or side to side.

HULL – the body or frame of a ship or boat.

INTACT – not broken or damaged.

MARVEL – something that is especially good or amazing to take in or look at.

PERMISSION – when a person in charge says it is okay to do something.

ROTOR – a part in a machine that rotates, or turns, inside another part.

VENTILATE – to allow fresh air to enter and move through a room.

Websites

To learn more about Cool Industrial Arts, visit **booklinks.abdopublishing.com**. These links are routinely monitored and updated to provide the most current information available.

INDEX